Prayer in Sadness & Sorrow

The healing power of Lament

by
Fr Robert Taylerson

*All booklets are published thanks to the
generous support of the members of the
Catholic Truth Society*

CATHOLIC TRUTH SOCIETY
PUBLISHERS TO THE HOLY SEE

Contents

Responding in prayer to anguish

When grief or anguish strikes, one of my natural reactions is to cry out from the heart. If the anguish is great then my reaction is from the depths of my being. My choice is not whether to respond, but simply how. This booklet introduces prayer of lament, which is profound response in prayer to anguish. The booklet also compares the positive turning to God with negative alternatives.

The starting point for prayer of lament is the experience of need or pain, acknowledging that this reduces what is human in us, our ability to interact with God and others. Lament is a faith-based healing journey which rehabilitates an individual or community. In the scriptures we see varied use of lament, not only concerning death. Even something lacking can be lamented, for example, Hannah lamenting her childlessness (1 *Sam* 1). In personal life we are called to lament our sins. In our world today we are encouraged to lament complex evils such as that of clerical sexual abuse. When should we lament? What is lament? Why is it important? How do we set about it?

Over a third of the biblical book of Psalms and much of the writing of the prophets is given to lament. Lament has its historical roots in death or the loss of one's previous way of life, being exiled or enslaved, but its use, its strength and power is far wider. Lament sometimes seems an almost-forgotten element of prayer in the Catholic tradition. It is however, I believe, one which is essential in Christian life. Here we explore its fuller nature and its rich and fruitful use in our lives today.

Christ has already come, so we might ask, "Is lament still appropriate?" It is true that as Christians we delight in Christ and give thanks for what he has done for us. Because his kingdom is not yet fully established, however, because sin, death and evil still have their influence in our world today, so lament continues to be a normal part of life. Now it goes hand in hand with thanks and with the knowledge that in Christ the victory is won. We are called to live by faith. This may include seeing beyond the current circumstances with the gift of hope which comes from God. Prayer of lament is often an integral element of that journey.

The Christian paradox is that it is normal for both lament and delight to be happening in our lives. Although I write here only about lament, it is my conviction that these two attitudes, two modes of prayer, delight and lament, should both have powerful places in our prayer lives.

When to lament

Am I faced with a major event which challenges hope? Is there an evil, a disaster or a trauma, a deep pain? Does God seem absent in these trials? Then is the time for prayer of lament. As our Christian journey continues, however, God may call us to compassion for others over an ever-widening range of circumstances. It is normal for prayer of lament to have broader boundaries as we continue on our Christian journey. So in day-to-day life I lament death and sickness of friends. I also lament break-ups of families. I lament the giving-up of the practice of the faith of many. I lament the problems of debt, of unemployment, of injustice, of sickness and stress. The call to find God in all things impels such prayer. To disregard lament would either allow so much to pile-up in my heart that hope would be crushed, or I would close the door to compassion. Lament is honest. Lament admits vulnerability. It doesn't pretend painful things don't happen. Neither does it pretend that I am to blame for all bad things I experience.

Lament is not to be thought of as one element in a well-equipped "spiritual toolkit"; as if life were like an engine, and its failing gearbox called for a spanner of a certain size to fix it... Death? Call for a novena to St Joseph, Hopeless cause? ... Call for St Rita or St Jude. Novenas, ritual prayers and other pious practices can play a powerful part in normal spiritual life, but lament does not fit in to such a category. The question "what is the process of lament?" calls for an answer which is not measured in any neat envelope of time nor fixed duration of ritual. The mystery and the personal interaction with God in lament can't be grasped if we limit our spiritual lives to prayers of a measured duration. Lament, like delight, should permeate our waking hours.

The prayer of lament is more deeply a journey, an inward transformation, never a "quick fix " of an experienced technician. It goes into the sadness or pain deep inside me, and there, paradoxically, eventually may discover God who is all love, God who is personal, God who made **me** in love. The circumstances of lament are such that its journey which starts with an emptiness, may discover that God, and only God, has the presence, the dimensions, the wholeness to fill the void. It is a journey from emptiness to grace by means of reborn hope. The distance to be travelled is unknown and like the Exodus of God's chosen people in scriptures parts of the journey may seem worse than the starting-point. And at the journey's end, even with God's all-filling light, the reality of the void may endure, but God is greater.

Neither will the lament journey allow me to focus solely on being an individual. It is too powerful to remain a selfish journey. However personal my anguish may be, however solitary the circumstances of my sadness appear, lament is a journey which turns my gaze on God and on others, and which redirects my gaze again and again through changing emotions, through challenges and weariness, through insights which often grow slower than any emerging plant from a seed, and it includes a gradual relinquishing of self, and an emerging simple trust in God.

What is prayer of lament?

The author Leo Tolstoy began his classic novel, Anna Karenina with the sentence, "All happy families resemble one another, each unhappy family is unhappy in its own way." It is an oft-quoted sentence because of the truth it contains about the personal nature of pain and anguish. No two experiences of unhappiness are the same.

The outpouring of joy in happiness is perceived as a more universal experience. The sadness of, for example, the death of *my* friend, the break-up of *our* family, the injustice done to *me*, the trials that we endure, is particular to me and a special community of which I am a part. Lament is about such personal or community unhappiness. It is about specific things which bring pain into our lives.

Lament responds to suffering by an emotional expression of that suffering. The absence which prompts lament is countered by an excess of expression, perhaps because what seemed to have meaning is no longer there. My behaviour, governed by the meaning and understanding of events, is at a loss, so goes beyond its normal boundaries.

At times, however, the anguish of others who are close to me may also draw me into lament. It is a mark of the depth of closeness to others when this happens. This is true not only of family and close friends, but also of a relationship with Jesus. Lamenting his suffering and death shows a personal relationship with him.

It is not whingeing

When I acknowledge a hurt then the response in me which needs to be triggered is that of lament. There is a profound difference between "whingeing" and "lamenting". Lament is open to my wound being examined. It is fully transparent. The complaint of a whinge is not. Lament is also a path of trust in vulnerability. A whinge more often derives from, and exhibits, hurt pride.

Clamour for God

Prayer of lament happens when I determinedly bring God into the picture. I deliberately and persistently tell him of the unhappiness over and over again, sharing one emotion after another, pleading one way then another, asking "why?", "how?", "when?" till I'm drained, using all the energy of my life to unite God with the object of unhappiness. Such is the starting-point of lament. It starts with a conviction that God must be involved, with a determination, with an energy often born out of desperation, but without either a full understanding of where the journey may lead or the routes to be taken. I may lament as an individual or as part of a body of people sharing the same pain. I clamour for God's attention and involvement.

It has some similarities to and some differences from petition. With prayer of petition a basic direction is this: When I have a conviction that something good is lacking, I pray to God asking for that good, and I continue to pray until one of two things happen. Either that good comes about, or God shows me clearly that his plan is for something else. Only when one of these outcomes arrives do I stop asking. Petition is simple and its aims can easily be understood.

Lament, however, starts elsewhere with the, "Out of the depths I cry to you, O Lord. Lord, hear my voice" (*Ps* 129/130), or similar sentiment. [*When quoting psalms I give both Greek and Hebrew numbering. 129 is Greek, 130 Hebrew*] The cry is more plaintive than eloquent. That shortest one-word prayer, "Help!" is at its root. It comes more from the heart than from the intellect, more from the spirit than the mind. Perhaps my rational self has already started to crumble, overwhelmed by the enormity of events. Perhaps my compassion, my grief or my fear of the unknown future seem to have eaten away all plans, hopes, and "normal" patterns of behaviour. It starts after a body-blow to myself or my community which has knocked the wind out of our sails.

Neither does lament have a fixed end-point. I have limited initial understanding of the direction in which it will lead, the view forwards only clarifies as the journey progresses. For the Christian the end-point often includes a deeper truth than Tolstoy's. That truth is one of incarnation and redemption. Jesus, though he doesn't explain all unhappiness, all sadness, or all horror, has come on earth to place himself in what is most empty, what is most without hope, what is most inhuman, most unhappy. Through love he is present in and redeems all unhappiness. All is united in him and transformed by him. A deepening of hope emerges. All will be well. Thus what grows in lament is the conviction of grace, the belief in God's help.

Lament is intrinsically unknowable in terms of its time scale. Lament of God's people in old-testament exile could be measured in generations. Lament of Martha, Mary and Jesus over the death of Lazarus lasted no more than four days. Because the nature of the hurt is particular, because God is our father, the interaction of lament between us and God does not come in any standard size or dimensions. It is part of the mystery of our life with God.

Prayer of lament starts with expression of human loss or pain, but it grows to encompass a conviction of grace already given or which will be given. The rendering of thanks to God is a sign of progress on the journey. Peace comes as the lament journey runs its course.

Harmful alternatives to lament

Prayer of lament is a dimension of belief in God, and there is an interrelationship between the two. As I lament, faith develops. As faith is present lament grows. Where there is pain, where there is faith, lament is in its element. Likewise prayer of lament is impossible if belief in God is rejected or denied.

The author G.K. Chesterton wrote that when men choose not to believe in God, they do not thereafter believe in nothing, but rather they then become capable of believing in anything. It seems to me that this is true with respect to lament. If God is abandoned, the reaction to a personal or community unhappiness is never "nothing", rather "anything" might be taken up.

So the presence of pain if God is not sought often leads to people taking other options. I suggest four common alternative directions to lament which may be adopted when suffering if faith is abandoned or not brought to bear on the pain. These four are: despair, anger, displacement activities, and bitterness.

Despair

The attraction of despair is that of the relinquishing of responsibility, claiming the freedom of not having to do anything, not having to work anything out. It is an attempt to shed a load which is too heavy to bear. Of all the alternatives to lament, however, it is the one which achieves nothing, which removes no pain, which has no power to lift, to heal, to grow.

Despair is the abandonment of hope. A conviction is grasped that nothing can be achieved, or that a task is too big to handle. Despair means allowing adversity to engulf all. Despair, because it is a rejection of both faith and hope, often includes a blindness to love. It puts up barriers to God's three highways of beauty, truth and love. It denies human fulfilment of an individual or a community. It is a dead end. It is merely an additional disease. Despair closes rather than opens the awareness of eternal life, of healing, of enduring love.

Do not imagine that the same outlook prompts lament and despair. It is true that the psalmist in lament cries out "My one companion is darkness" (*Ps* 87/88). If he were despairing this would be a complacent proclamation. As he is lamenting it is a cry of anguish and complaint. Where there is a hurt, don't give up on anguish.

Anger

The emotion of anger brings with it a variety of changes in our behaviour. It can seem attractive because it may bring with it a certain optimism. Anger often entails a change of perspective which seems dynamic. Indeed scriptural scenes such as Jesus driving money-changers out of the temple, or Psalm four, which speaks of a trembling (usually understood as with anger) but not sinning, show that at least some of the attributes of anger can on occasion be good. Likewise the energy to bring about justice can start with the hurt which injustice sparks in me. This sense of injustice is a form of anger, and can result in good. Many changes have been brought about in society by what started out as a sense of injustice.

The evil side of anger, however, is also shown in changes of our attitudes and behaviour. Where anger is aggressive its symptoms are destructiveness, hurtfulness selfishness, vengeance, bullying and the like. Where anger is passive, attitudes to people can become evasive, obsessive, manipulative or similar. Anger tries to blind its owners to the evils which are a general consequence of its unleashing.

So the initial unhappiness or the pain of an individual or community is rarely helped but is often compounded by the changes in attitude and behaviour brought about by anger. Often anger introduces more hurt, more evil.

Anger, too, is often accompanied by resistance to compassion, resistance to seeing one's own faults, blindness to beauty. Anger and thankfulness don't mix, and until I am once more capable of giving thanks my life is still broken.

Displacement activities

A displacement activity is that which tries to fill the mind with an alternative to what has caused the hurt or has made people unhappy. This, too, seems attractive, and may have good elements. For instance, our English word, "Gossip" is thought to have derived from "Good Sib" ...good sibling. The background being that when a woman is in labour, giving birth, a "good sister" would be at her side telling her harmless tittle-tattle to distract her mind from the pain of childbirth. The real pain of childbirth, which in this case is hopefully temporary, is alleviated by filling the mind with trivia so the pain has less effect.

The long-term distraction of gossip more commonly, however, is evil because it often shares scandal or invites one to dwell on enticing thoughts of vice. It binds the mind, the will, and the perception in a way which causes further harm to individual or community.

We know, too, that distraction from pain is not a good permanent state in which to live, as pain is a way of telling us that something is not right, something needs healing. It needs attention. Displacements try to mask this truth, and create for us an alternative world of shadows, of distractions in which we try to live, but can never be fully alive, never be healed.

Displacement activities come in many forms. An early indicator that they may be present is when solitary silence is deliberately removed from one's daily timetable. (For that is where the soul most naturally cries out to God, and listens to God's whispers in return).

With displacement alternative dramas are welcomed. One doesn't have to be a character in an internet world, nor have the virtual personality of an avatar. Sometimes an absorption with TV soaps or sports or music can attempt to provide a barrier to awareness of the deep hurt within. "Being busy" is a state into which energies are alternatively put. Efforts are made to create a structure which attempts a stability, a shell, or barrier to vulnerability. Personal conversations at a level deeper than passing the time of day are shunned. Occasions which trigger compassion for real people (as opposed to virtual characters) are avoided. Deepest hurts are locked in a cupboard. Life is unexamined.

Though often less destructive than anger, no release from pain is possible, it constantly lies beneath the surface.

Bitterness

Bitterness is an action of personal autonomy. That is its attraction. My human dignity is felt to have been infringed and this is something I can do in redress. Through bitterness I assert myself.

Bitterness against people is often associated with a sense that they have betrayed us. Bitterness with God is similar. "Look, God, I thought we had a deal ... I'd be good and in return you would give me a life free of pain!" What happens in me when pain appears is a seething resentment, frustration, hatred and a wish that if my life has grown bitter, all others' lives should at least be bitter too. The outburst to God is "If this is how you treat me, I'm not going to believe in you anymore!"

Like other vices the spirits which propose it to us always cast our thoughts to the middle distance, to stereotypes, to assumed motives, and away from compassion, away from a sense of our shared sinfulness away from understanding others as persons.

Bitterness comes when awareness of the effects of original sin and actual sin are unexamined. The reality of good and evil in the world are not acknowledged in daily life. Bitterness is not something of an instant or of the crest of a wave. Its roots for Christians may even lie in the false comfort of seeing religion in its laws, and missing the loving Jesus who takes sin on himself and asks us to follow. Breaking of bitterness can't be achieved by a call which says, "Get Real!", but only by an experience of love. And bitterness, unforgiveness, and the barriers they construct always try to stop love getting through.

Self-awareness and discernment

In my own life I have sometimes turned away from the path of lament in favour of each of these alternatives, which, on occasions, I have chosen. Through a personal history of right and wrong choices I gradually learn that there is always a need for discernment which combines honesty, vulnerability, and awareness of self and community. Each day I need to be honest about pain, loss or unhappiness in my life, as each day I reaffirm trust in God. When I acknowledge that pain is present then my antennae need to be up. How easily I can be seduced by the attractions of despair, anger, displacement activities and bitterness. The identification of these so often flags up the missing element of lament which should be active in my life. That is why lament too often is delayed in my own life, after I take steps down one of the four cul-de-sacs.

I see this too in the lives of others. How tragic it is when someone suffers the loss of a loved one, then takes on the response of long-term anger. The first evil (death) is compounded by the second and two knots of emotion, two oppressions have taken the place of one. Likewise how sad it is when a husband walks out on wife and family and they then take on the mantle of bitterness, perhaps to be worn for the next fifty years or more. The utter compounding of evil casts shadows over so many.

Of course, going down any of the four cul-de-sacs can occur without the trigger of hurt. They are vices which can seem attractive under many circumstances. It is good to be aware of their attractions in day-to-day life regardless of any hurt which may or may not be present in my life. However it seems to me that their attraction in times of hurt is very strong, and the questions "Are they present?" and "Should lament be happening?" are wise ones to ask in tandem.

In a world dominated by questions such as "Do I have possessions ... things?" or "How up-to-date/fashionable am I?", the fog can too easily be drawn over central questions which lead to fullness of life. The questions "Do I have joy?" and "Do I have sadness?" cut to the point. If I am sad then "Do I have hope?" becomes a key question. Perhaps I need to learn this lesson again and again to stop arrogance, autonomy, self-satisfaction and so many other comfortable habits from gaining the upper hand.

Grief and lament

In the New Testament most of the direct references concerning lament refer to grief. It is, too, a central starting point for lament in much of the Hebrew scriptures. Grief makes us cry out "Why" at a gut level. Faith makes us cry out "Why" in prayer of lament, yet there are not two "why's" but one. My life of grace is not divorced from my natural life.

Over the last forty years theories have abounded coming from the human sciences about what is normal in human grief (and in facing death). Perhaps the best-known is that of Elisabeth Kubler-Ross, suggesting that a sequence of denial, anger, bargaining, depression, then acceptance, is common. There is an understanding that many people work through grief in similar ways, though individuals also vary widely in their personal journeys.

For people of faith, a great simplicity and transparency of grief is often present in scriptural lament. When king David's wayward son Absalom dies, David cries out... "And the king was much moved, and went up to the upper chamber of the gate, and wept; and as he went, he said: O my son Absalom, my son, my son Absalom! would God I had died in your stead, O Absalom, my son, my son!" (2 *Sam* 18:33).

Looking through secular texts on grieving, and comparing them with scriptural texts on lament several differences, are clear. With faith vulnerability stays more at the surface. The re-living of the blessings of someone's life also more frequently gives rise to thanks. The sense "I should be in control" which can lead to bitterness in grief, is seen to be false, and the helplessness of a child (of God) is understood as real.

With faith I am invited to enter into a full mystery of death. I feel it personally, but also come to know God's presence in it, and I grow in understanding of Christ's death too.

Lamenting sin

It takes a gift, a grace from God to enable prayer of lament to happen in my life. When God blesses me with just a glimpse (I could not stand the full vision) of the true effects of my sin, that gift is the trigger. Sin causes such hurt. If I were to realise the full hurt of sin, it would break me apart. Lament of sin happens when I recognise, or am open to becoming aware of the evil of my sin. I can then see sin as a death, as an exile, as a slavery. Lament of sin comes with a clarity of vision. Sin and sadness go together. Three attitudes can get in the way, however, of a "good sadness" for sin: unbalanced guilt, seeing sin as bland, and the thought ...why bother?

Unbalanced guilt

Sometimes my sense of guilt is strong. Sometimes it is balanced, sometimes not. As a child I remember schoolteachers, nuns and clergy who could instil a sense of guilt in me when I'd done nothing wrong! That potential is still present in my life.

Likewise if sin becomes a habit, my conscious awareness of it diminishes. It can sink beneath the radar of my self perception. No sense of sin is apparent in my conscious awareness (though sin always harms my freedom) and no guilt or pain at all is felt. What I don't see or sense, I have no guilt over.

Likewise occasionally into my mind will come a flashback of sins of the past, which have already been forgiven after repentance and sacramental reconciliation. It is as if that sin were fresh on my conscience once more. It may preoccupy my mind. When the prophet Micah talks about "To the bottom of the sea God throws all my sins," (*Micah* 7:19) when Christ talks about forgiveness, it is clear that such "fishing for past, forgiven sins" is not a healthy pastime. Should sin flashbacks occur, ideally they should prompt in me renewed joy in their being forgiven, then be put aside. Being enslaved by memories of forgiven sins is an oppression.

Seeing sin as bland

Often I am aware that I have sinned, but don't have a strong consciousness of the evil of it. I may even try to develop a life vision that denies the true nature of sin, asking God to "overlook my mistakes" rather than begging his forgiveness for sin. The psalms give a range of advice in their laments, "Make me know the shortness of my life, that I may gain wisdom of heart"

(*Ps* 38/39) or "I remember the days that are past; I ponder all your works" (*Ps* 142/143). Asking for the tools of reflection, for the tools of insight is often needed. It is good to come to God with "I don't know…" for then he can teach me It is good to ask to be taught …He will.

The thought … Why bother thinking about sin?

The lamenting of sin is a blessing for me, rather than for God. The more I am aware of its horror, the more I will have the strength to avoid it. The sense of sin is a tremendous blessing. For me it makes the understanding of Jesus' sacrifice and his victory over sin all the more wonderful. Lament of sin has the reverse effect to what one might expect. Yes it starts in a growing horror of what I have done, but it doesn't keep me sad, doesn't keep me fearful, rather it is a pathway which sets me free and makes me thankful.

I find lament for sin sometimes has unexpected outcomes. It can give me a drive to do, in particular, acts of quiet generosity and virtue, to respond well. It may enable me to be patient when visiting those whose minds are feeble and ask me the same question for the fifth time in so many minutes. It can help me with the aggressive beggar at the door, or with the tense meeting where no-one shares a vision with another, with the day-to-day petty injustices, dishonesties and knocks of life. The awareness gained through lament for sin ...yes I too partake of the evil in this world, I am an accomplice, I too need redemption ... gives a strength, hard to find elsewhere, to make a Christian response.

Lamenting
complex evil

In addition to individual evils our world today has more complex evils, hurts, and causes of unhappiness. A clear case in point is the recent plethora of cases of clerical sexual abuse. We are asked to lament this. Our Church, however, lacks a tradition of prayer of lament for issues which are both evil and complex.

When called to "lament clerical sexual abuse" how do I set about it? A similar question could be asked of any systematic injustice, oppression or abuse. What is certain is that here is a set of multiple tragedies, multiple evils. The tragedy of an innocent person being the victim of a sexual predator is real. The tragedy of betrayal of trust is real. The tragedy of cover-ups, which block justice and facilitate perpetuation of evil is real. The structure which encourages or forms a warped or distorted understanding of "avoidance of scandal" is real, and so on. The shock is not only one of individual sin, it is one of discovering that the Church, a body of which I am part, lacks a needed internal awareness of and reaction to this evil. Like any evil, like any pain, first

I take it to God crying out "Why", "How" again and again with each aspect of the evil. It brings reflection on power, responsibility, accountability … it calls for a clear vision of truth, of where evil lies and so on.

In practice I lament different aspects separately. I can't bring it all together in one vision. I know those who have been abused by priests and I lament their predation. I know some of those who have been abusers and I lament the evil they have done. I know those who have been brought up in a system where senior clergy thought they were doing right by reprimanding abusers, accepting pleas of their repentance and moving them elsewhere. I lament those systems. I know families who have experienced the deep hurt of betrayal in finding that those clergy who abused their children had been appointed following suspicions or knowledge of abuse elsewhere. I lament the hurt they suffer.

I also know priests who under the current safeguarding policies have been removed from their home, their friends, their livelihoods at the first accusation (which may or may not have foundation) and have been in a limbo of suspension. I have seen the reduction in youth activities in schools and churches as checks, regulations and restrictions have increased. These too I lament. And so I could continue.

The more complex the evil, the more I have to pray about, the more I am called to realise the way in which one evil predisposes another evil to take place. This awareness prompts in me a desire and petition for deeper insight, deeper honesty, deeper compassion, more detailed personal examination of conscience and discernment of motives in my own life, more courageous action against evil, more trusting confidence in God alone.

Learning to lament

We are blessed as Catholics in our tradition. Here we find ways to train ourselves in prayer of lament. Some habitual pious exercises e.g. the sorrowful mysteries of the rosary, and stations of the cross, are taught to us as children. Praying psalms is more likely an adult habit, as is reflective reading of other scripture texts. We are encouraged to pray them not simply as habitual pious exercises for the sake of it. They help to form in our hearts attitudes for love, for service, for personal prayer, for trust in God, for the recognition and acknowledgement of evil. It is the awareness of pain, of hurt or unhappiness which prompts in me the stirring of compassion. This makes these prayers deeper for me and provides the right experience from which I can start to lament well. When the depth of these is experienced then they become our personal lessons to guide us through our own hurts and those of our community. They educate me for prayer of lament. In scripture too not only the Psalms but many parts of the Old Testament are full of teachings on lament. Good examples are the book of the prophet Jeremiah (and its associated poems of the book of Lamentations), the books of Job, Habakkuk and Amos.

Praying the Prayer of the Church daily is a tradition of priests, religious brothers and sisters and an increasing number of laypeople. This includes many psalms of lament and old testament canticles of lament. By using it large numbers of people may pray between ten and fifteen scriptural laments each week.

Central in the fruits of our tradition is the hope-renewing journey of prayer of lament. We must take it as individuals and as community again and again. Where there is grief, anguish and evil then a loving response is lament. You and I are made in the image of God, this image of love. Where there is anguish we are drawn into lament in the depths of our being. The deepest journey of lament is always a journey of love.

Lament in the Old Testament

L ament is widespread in the Old Testament. At the back of this booklet are details of books by scholars who have considered scriptural lament in great detail. They give suggestions about the way in which laments unfold in the scriptures. I mention here a couple of their models. For greater detail please look at the books in the bibliography.

One suggestion is that the lament process has three elements to it. First is *invocation*, in which the one praying makes it clear that he or she is determined to involve God at all costs in the particular sorrow. Second is the *lament* itself. This never contains elements of resignation or submission, but rather asks God piercing questions, especially "Why?" The words often come out as complaint or protest. Third is the element of *petition*. This is integral to lament because without it lament could become a meditation on suffering. With it the sense of appeal to God is prominent. In this are the seeds of trust and hope. In it is the personal relationship with God which develops as the journey progresses.

This triple model fits well with the strong characters of Jeremiah and Job, two great teachers of lament. They call on God again and again. Their dialogue for ages seems to be one-sided. God seems not to hear them or to ignore them. Jeremiah and Job come through as steadfast, as growing in maturity through the long encounters and as witnesses not only of lament, but also of that trust and hope which is the outcome of lament. What happens to individuals also happens to communities. Examples are in the Exodus (Numbers 11 to 21) and in the prophets, e.g. Amos 4.

Another way of looking at lament concerns theodicy. This is the area of theology which looks at the goodness of God, the freedom of man, the nature of evil and the attaining of justice. Where lament is considered in these terms the nature of the suffering or evil can be described in one of three categories; first as *deserved suffering* or punishment e.g. for sin, second as seemingly *innocent suffering*, and third as a sub-category of the latter, *redemptive suffering*. Clearly redemptive suffering brings to mind Our Lord's own suffering on the cross for us all. These three categories are useful in trying to understand one's own suffering. Indeed when lament becomes intense we are almost obliged to try to fit our personal experiences into one of these understandings.

Where, for example, personal sin is repented of, God is clearly just and the ideal response of the sufferer is one of recognition and acknowledgement of sin. Psalm 50/51, with its phrases "My offences, truly I know them" and God "being justified when he gives sentence" stand witness to the way in which deserved punishment can clarify personal examination of conscience and awareness of sin. The two great instances of i. awareness of an evil or a punishment resulting from sin and ii. the awareness of how much God loves me, are the most powerful ways of shedding light on my personal sinfulness. The identification of redemptive suffering in laments is found clearly in the book of Job and in the suffering servant songs in the book of Isaiah (*Isa* 50:4-11 and 52:13-53:12). The lament of undeserved suffering is found in the Pentateuch (e.g. *Gen* 18:22-33; *Exod* 32:7-14; *Num* 11:4-13) in the prophets, especially Jeremiah and Habakkuk, in the Psalms of lament and elsewhere. The scriptures provide us with events, emotions and relationships for us to compare with our own.

Lament in the Psalms

Psalm 21/22 is the most excessive of all psalms in its lament. The number of woes exceed that which could be imagined. Fierce bulls of Bashan, like lions, many dogs tearing holes in me, the sword, the band of the wicked, the parched throat, disjointed bones, melted heart, the protruding bones, those who stare and gloat and cast lots for my clothes, all this and more beset the lamenter. This is the psalm which Jesus starts praying in his passion. Perhaps because there are so many woes it is easier to bring to mind when we are overwhelmed. Psalm 21/22 is also a typical psalm of the type where the pendulum swings between anguish and hope. It gives one reason for lament after another, then also proclaims God as the psalmist's "Praise in the great assembly" (Ps 21/22:26). Other psalms of individual lament show no respite in anguish and little hope. An example of what seems total bleakness is Psalm 87/88 which starts by calling God's help by day and night and concludes with the awareness that the psalmist's one companion is darkness. Psalms of individual lament are the most numerous of any category of psalms, numbering about forty. Their approach and content vary widely. They include cries that one has been falsely accused (e.g. Ps 7), confessions of guilt (e.g. Ps 50/51), and protestations of innocence (e.g. Ps 25/26). In addition to the individual laments are the communal laments, another ten or more psalms, where the community pray together in the light of a disaster or shared grief.

Reflection on the shortness of human life (*Ps* 89/90), a cry for communal humility (*Ps* 122/123), and the cry of homesickness by the rivers of Babylon (*Ps* 136/137), are all emotive constant reminders of the reality of suffering. They give a range of ways in which people lament, but always draw God into the centre, always trust, always acknowledge that God is deeper than human frailties.

Lament in the New Testament

When, in Mark's gospel (*Mk* 15:34) Jesus laments, he is shown doing so using the words of Psalm 21/22, "My God, why have you forsaken me?" He uses the psalms to lament in a way which is at the heart of the Jewish prayer tradition. He makes the lament of his people his own.

The understanding of events of suffering and our prayer response from scripture is, however much more widespread. Many Catholic authors have written on it and on associated topics such as suffering. As examples, I offer here some brief reflections of Blessed Pope John Paul II, and St Augustine.

Blessed Pope John Paul II

In his 1984 encyclical on suffering, *Salvifici Doloris*, Blessed John Paul starts as follows:

Declaring the power of salvific suffering, the Apostle Paul says: "In my flesh I complete what is lacking in Christ's afflictions for the sake of his body, that is, the Church". These words seem to be found at the end of the long road that winds through the suffering which forms part of the history of man and which is illuminated by the Word of God. These words have as it were the value of a final discovery, which is accompanied by joy. For this reason Saint Paul writes: "Now I rejoice in my sufferings for your sake". The joy comes from the discovery of the meaning of suffering, and this discovery, even if it is most personally shared in by Paul of Tarsus who wrote these words, is at the same time valid for others. The Apostle shares his own discovery and rejoices in it because of all those whom it can help—just as it helped him—to understand *the salvific meaning of suffering*.

John Paul takes us down the path which helps us to find God in suffering. He sees suffering as something intrinsic to the human state and describes it as:

It is as deep as man himself, precisely because it manifests in its own way that depth which is proper to man, and in its own way surpasses it. Suffering seems to belong to man's transcendence: it is one of those points in which man is in a certain sense "destined" to go beyond himself, and he is called to this in a mysterious way.

John Paul sees scripture as rich in detail of human suffering:

> Sacred Scripture is a *great book about suffering*. Let us quote from the books of the Old Testament a few examples of situations which bear the signs of suffering, and above all moral suffering: the danger of death, the death of one's own children and, especially, the death of the firstborn and only son; and then too: the lack of offspring, nostalgia for the homeland, persecution and hostility of the environment, mockery and scorn of the one who suffers, loneliness and abandonment; and again: the remorse of conscience, the difficulty of understanding why the wicked prosper and the just suffer, the unfaithfulness and ingratitude of friends and neighbours; and finally: the misfortunes of one's own nation.

In the above he sums up the sorrows of mankind. Although he doesn't follow this by a discourse on lament, this collection of woes sums up perhaps better than any other the range of woes which are lamented in scripture. By reference to the Gospels he also shows how Jesus himself drew ever closer to the world of human suffering:

> In his messianic activity in the midst of Israel, Christ drew increasingly closer *to the world of*

human suffering. "He went about doing good", and his actions concerned primarily those who were suffering and seeking help. He healed the sick, consoled the afflicted, fed the hungry, freed people from deafness, from blindness, from leprosy, from the devil and from various physical disabilities, three times he restored the dead to life. He was sensitive to every human suffering, whether of the body or of the soul. And at the same time he taught, and at the heart of his teaching there are *the eight beatitudes*, which are addressed to people tried by various sufferings in their temporal life. These are "the poor in spirit" and "the afflicted" and "those who hunger and thirst for justice" and those who are "persecuted for justice sake", when they insult them, persecute them and speak falsely every kind of evil against them for the sake of Christ... Thus according to Matthew; Luke mentions explicitly those "who hunger now".

At any rate, Christ drew close above all to the world of human suffering through the fact of having taken *this suffering upon his very self.* During his public activity, he experienced not only fatigue, homelessness, misunderstanding even on the part of those closest to him, but, more than anything, he became progressively more and more isolated and encircled by hostility and the preparations for putting him to death.

In this great teaching on suffering blessed John Paul helps us to put our own experiences of suffering in right perspective, the perspective of Christ. When we do this hope grows.

St Augustine

St Augustine of Hippo wrote many works. In his expositions on psalms (*enarrationes in psalmos*) he sees Christ foretold in the psalms. He sees the loss depicted in the lament psalms as helping us to realise the deeper loss when we separate ourselves from Christ, when we fail in love and in zeal. (These understandings are explained in greater depth in the article by Brian Brock, details of which are given in the bibliography). In his commentary on Psalm 101/102 Augustine notes that many people lament for poor reasons (such as the loss of money) but fail to lament for more serious reasons such as the loss of faith. The fact that we are so attached to earthly things that we may lament their loss he sees as itself a cause for lament. He teaches us to strongly treasure the treasures of faith and to deeply lament their loss when they are absent. In his commentary on Psalm 85/86 he looks at the beatitude "blessed are those who mourn" and suggests that the "blessedness" is in hope as the "mourning" is in current awareness and in action. In one sense all our earthly life contains mourning as we await Christ's return. Lament equates with yearning for Christ's second coming. Likewise Augustine calls his readers again and again to regard Christ's own suffering. In our own laments we turn our minds to the suffering Christ. As Christ prayed from the cross and was seemingly unanswered, so may we be too. As Christ was deeply loved by the Father in this, so too may we be.

St Augustine and Blessed John Paul II are good teachers to help us to recognise where evil or sadness are real. The help us to achieve a Christian perspective in discerning what is truly a cause for anguish and what is not. They lead us down good paths of prayer which establish in out hearts lament, hope and trust in God. They give us confidence to cry out to God when our experiences are bleak, and to recognise that the New Testament scriptures, as well as the Old Testament, give us sound teachings in lament.

My own realisation, both coming from their wisdom and from the praying of psalms over many years, is of the need to lament over events and occasions of sadness which I would previously not have taken to prayer. To grow in compassion is to grow in vulnerability to sharing pain, distress, and sadness. For the Christian the teacher for that growth is Jesus, himself. So authentic growth in compassion will include being drawn deeper into association with Christ on the cross as well as deeper sharing in others' pain. The added reflection of Augustine that the time from the Ascension to the second coming of Christ is a time of "yearning" is also helpful to me.

What about tears?

The phrase "the gift of tears" is thought to have first come into Christian spiritual writing in a work attributed to St Athanasius (who died 373 AD), but the sense that tears are a part of spiritual life, and may be there for God's purpose is much older. Prayers with tears are an accepted part of ancient Jewish tradition. They are found in Old Testament and New Testament scripture. From the spiritual writings of the early Greek and Syriac speaking Christian Church onwards, tears to accompany Christian prayer have also been seen as normal, and tears to accompany prayers of repentance have often been seen as a gift from God. First I want to look at tears simply as a human phenomenon. Following this I will look at scripture and then the later Christian tradition of spiritual writing on tears.

Tears in humanity

Tears are only partly under the control of our wills. Our emotions also play a part. These can facilitate our tears and powerful emotions can cause them to be more abundant. Negative emotions can bring about tears of anger, revolt, rage or despair. Emotions associated with awareness of something lacking can promote tears on occasions of sadness, affliction, depression or homesickness. Powerful vices such as jealousy or pride can promote tears. Aspects of personal vulnerability can promote tears. These show in pity or compassion for others, or being overwhelmed aesthetically by something of great beauty, or something or deep horror. Young children cry when they don't get their own way, when they are exhausted and when they get scared, and although these circumstances don't usually bring about tears in adults, they can contribute with other factors to help tears to flow.

Tears often mark and point to the values which are a deep part of my existence. They can show me and others how much we value what is now lost or how much we have sadness at what may never be attained. They can indicate where there is a horror, or what is seen as menacing. What they show is not a philosophy of mind, but rather what I hold dear from my heart, my spirit, my soul. Authentic tears are often spontaneous and can express sincere affections. They are a means of communication firstly to ourselves. What may be a shock of bursting into tears always has something to teach me about what is happening in my life. Tears are also a means of communication with others. They have a power in showing empathy, pity, sympathy, and deep bonds of love or friendship which can be profound and strong.

Tears in Scripture

There are many occasions of tears being shed in the scriptures. Indeed often I would find it odd in some biblical scenes if the combination of people and circumstance didn't merit tears. A good place to start observing is in the book of Psalms. Here we find tears of the just in distress, tears of those persecuted by enemies, tears of those facing death, tears of those in exile, those in repentance and much more. Some of the best-known snapshots of weeping are as follows: "every night I drench my pillow with tears" (*Ps* 6:7), "my tears have become my bread day and night" (*Ps* 41/42:3), "The bread I eat is ashes, my drink, mingled with tears" (*Ps* 101/102:9), "You (God) fed them (your people) with tears for their bread, abundance of tears for their drink" (*Ps* 79/80), "O Lord turn your ear to my cry, do not be deaf to my tears" (*Ps* 38/39:12), "By the rivers of Babylon, there we sat and wept remembering Zion" (*Ps* 136/137). The regular praying of psalms holds a mirror to my own life and challenges those norms of society which might suggest it is not the done thing to weep.

Elsewhere in the Hebrew scriptures (e.g. 2 *Kings* 20:5) we see God telling his people that he has seen their tears and is responding to them. The response of God to human tears is no different to the loving human response to tears, to that of a parent, a friend, or a lover.

In the gospels we see the woman who had sinned weeping (*Lk* 38:44) and we see Peter weeping when he denied Jesus (*Mt* 26:75, *Mk* 14:72, *Lk* 22:62). Tears of repentance are to be encouraged. We see Jesus weeping at the tomb of Lazarus (*Jn* 11:35) and weeping for Jerusalem, for its infidelity and future collapse (*Lk* 19:41). The letter to the Hebrews describes Jesus' offering himself for us as follows "In the days of his flesh Jesus offered up prayers and supplications with loud cries and tears" (*Heb* 5:7). This is a reminder of the fullness with which Jesus gave himself for us in his passion and death.

Some of the circumstances of tears give us more to ponder over and are less clear. Luke's version of the beatitudes shows Jesus saying that those who cry now are happy for they will laugh (*Lk* 6:21), a more stark proclamation than Matthew's gospel which simply says that the mourners are happy for they will be consoled (*Mt* 5:4). Luke's beatitude may bring to mind St Augustine's understanding that in the era between Christ's Ascension and his second coming there is an element of lament in Christian life as we await his return. The promise of Isaiah (*Is* 25:8) which is repeated in the book of Revelation (*Rev* 7:17) that the Lord God will wipe away the tears from our eyes, can also be understood as referring to our yearning for Christ's second coming.

Very often where darkness or judgement and condemnation is referred to in the gospels it is described as a place where there is weeping and grinding of teeth (*Mt* 8:12, 13:42 etc.). This pictures well the misery of an eternity separated from God. Other depictions of tears encourage the virtue of empathy, such as St Paul's encouragement that we should "weep with those who weep" (*Rom* 12:15).

One way to understand tears in a spiritual light is by using the scriptures. As with all scriptures asking the question "why" is often fruitful. Spending time praying through the passages of scripture which mention tears can give us spiritual insight into our own, and sometimes help us to recognise spiritual friends among the holy men and women of old.

Tears in Christian writings

There is a wealth of spiritual writing on tears by early monks of the Eastern Christian tradition. Arsenius the hermit (4th Century) was seen as a hero because he wept so much ... all through his working day, every day. The English word "compunction" implies having one's peace "pierced" by awareness of personal sin, and the older Greek word "penthos" carries with it similar overtones. Many spiritual writers who wrote in Greek and Syriac (Evagrius, Ephraem, Gregory of Nazianzen, Dorotheus of Gaza, Basil, Theodore the Studite, John

Chrysostom and others) assumed that, with God's grace, tears were frequently associated with compunction. They took tears as the norm for those who were seriously sorry for sins, were deeply aware of Jesus giving himself for them personally on the cross, and yearned that both themselves and others be freed from sin. Several also assumed that praying about death, judgement, heaven and hell would promote tears in those who were serious about such prayer. Several writers used allegories of baptism to indicate that tears of compunction associated with prayer had power to free a person from sin.

One author's set of images I find helpful to reflect on is that of the early fifth-century monk, John the Solitary. He suggested that tears flow from us for different reasons. He suggests three different starting-points (three different types of person) and lists the thoughts which provoke tears to flow for each.

The bodily man has cares and concerns for children, home possessions, memory of misfortunes and deceased relatives.

The mental man has fear of judgement, conscience, death etc.

The Spiritual man has awe of God's wisdom, his majesty etc., (all tears coming not from sadness, but joy.)

John's three categories are one way to help assess where my deepest values and concerns are at any given time. (John also elsewhere suggested that when human minds dwell in the spiritual realm then tears may cease as men become more like the angels who do not cry.)

As the spiritual tradition of the monks of the Eastern Christian Churches developed the understanding of the way in which tears can be a gift which accompanies prayer grew. With time there was also the caution not to assume that simply because there are tears, the spiritual life is progressing and deepening. John Climacus (579-649) in the seventh chapter of his *Ladder of Divine Ascent* strikes a good balance. He upholds the teaching that tears especially of compunction accompany prayers well, but also cautions against the "one-upmanship" which those who weep in prayer can claim, and calls all to examine their hearts more than their tears. This was a much-needed counsel to govern the more exaggerated claims concerning spiritual tears and the sense of spiritual competition in weeping which was growing in some monastic circles. The underlying teaching that tears often serve a powerful purpose of God, however is upheld by all.

In the Western Christian Church John Cassian (365 - 435) was the first to describe different reasons for tears. He did this in the ninth of his conferences (IX, 28-30).

Compunction, the thought of past sins is a common reason. Joy in the Lord also promotes tears, as does longing for the glory of eternity. Fear of hell can promote tears, as can awareness of the sins and hard-heartedness of others. The anxieties of life too may play a part. Cassian taught that forced or squeezed-out tears, though they may come from zeal to be penitent, have less value than spontaneous prayers. St Benedict (480-547) in his rule, much of which includes Cassian's wisdom, mentions tears several times as a natural accompaniment to prayer (RB IV,57 ; LII, 4; XX,3). Gregory the Great (540-604), in his *Dialogues* (III,34) has similar teaching.

In medieval times many spiritual writers included teaching on tears. St Bernard and subsequent Cistercian writers considered tears for personal sin and for future beatitude, and saw them as giving strength for the Christian journey. Aelred of Rievaulx (1110 -1167) wrote a very helpful account of a novice who had previously wept in compunction for his sins, but on entering the monastery those tears has dried up. He was anxious and feared that this marked a backward step in his relationship with God. Aelred questioned him, found him devout and prayerful, and saw the tears as having been a grace for previous life, and it was God's will that they were not to be currently shed. (*The*

Mirror of Charity 2,17). The same questioning and reassurance would be of help to many today who are in a similar situation.

Tears, too at times were a focus of popular piety. The eleventh century Salve Regina (Hail Holy Queen) with its "vale of tears" and the thirteenth century Stabat Mater with "At the cross her station keeping stood the mournful mother, weeping", bear witness to this.

In the later spiritual writings of the saints, St Teresa of Avila (1515-1582), takes it for granted that tears accompany prayer at various stages of spiritual life (*Life* Chap 10,14,19 *Way of Perfection* Chap 19). Teresa starts off (Chap 10) by seeing tears as a mark of tenderness, promoted by love. They are also a treasured gift from God. She next sees tears as an accompaniment to progress in prayer (Ch 14) but here joy predominates rather than sorrow. In Chapter 19, discussing the union with God in prayer, she recounts how her tears gush following the experience of such union. Teresa is at a loss to explain it well. (She tries, but then suggests she might be talking gibberish!) But she is convinced that this course of prayer and commitment to it must be pursued.

St Ignatius of Loyola (1491-1556) sometimes cried so much at Mass that he could not continue. He was afraid that the gift of tears might lead to loss of eyesight. In his *Spiritual Exercises* he expects tears to be normally associated with penance (*Ex.* 87) and with meditation on Christ's passion (*Ex.* 195). I have followed St Ignatius' Exercises in 30 day retreats twice and my own experience and those of many who have made such retreats is that God's love and guidance in matters central to the retreat journey are often accompanied by tears of the retreatant. The intensity of the focus on Christ and the awareness of God's personal love and call are powerful in a way which brings them about.

It is clear from the scriptures and the Christian tradition that tears should not be dismissed as unimportant. God clearly uses them in his plan for us and they can be a means of grace. At the same time they are not necessarily a touchstone of authenticity, of grief or sorrow, nor of union with Christ in his suffering, nor should their starting or stopping in our lives be a cause for concern. Praying with and learning from the holy men and women in our history is good practice. Beyond that God made us individuals and calls us to show love, concern and sorrow through different ways in different individuals. They are both a means of God's guidance and an invitation for us to express our love.

Conclusion

Prayer of lament is a journey of the heart from anguish to peace. Though its path is not immediately obvious, it is a path of God's love and it is a grace and a source of hope. Always ask for the courage and trust to take it.

Bibliography

Scripture quotes in this booklet are from the CTS Bible
SC101 - *CTS New Catholic Bible - Standard Edition*
Do 555 - *Salvifici Doloris*

A good collection of theological essays on lament, from a variety of authors and denominations is to be found in:

Evoking Lament edited by Eva Harasta & Brian Brock, Continuum, Published by T&T Clark London 2009.
(This includes the excellent essay on St Augustine by Brian Brock, and essays which expound the different scriptural lament models given in this booklet)

The Gift of the Psalms Roland E Murphy O Carm., Hendrickson publishers. Peabody., Mass. USA. 2000.
(Many commentaries on Psalms have good teachings on Psalms of lament. I used several in researching this booklet. One good simple commentary I would recommend is this one)

Dictionnaire de Spiritualite (Beauchesne, Paris) Adnes, P. *Larmes* DS Tome IX (1976) col 287-303.
(For details on "Tears" a good article, containing much greater detail than I have given here, is found in the above)